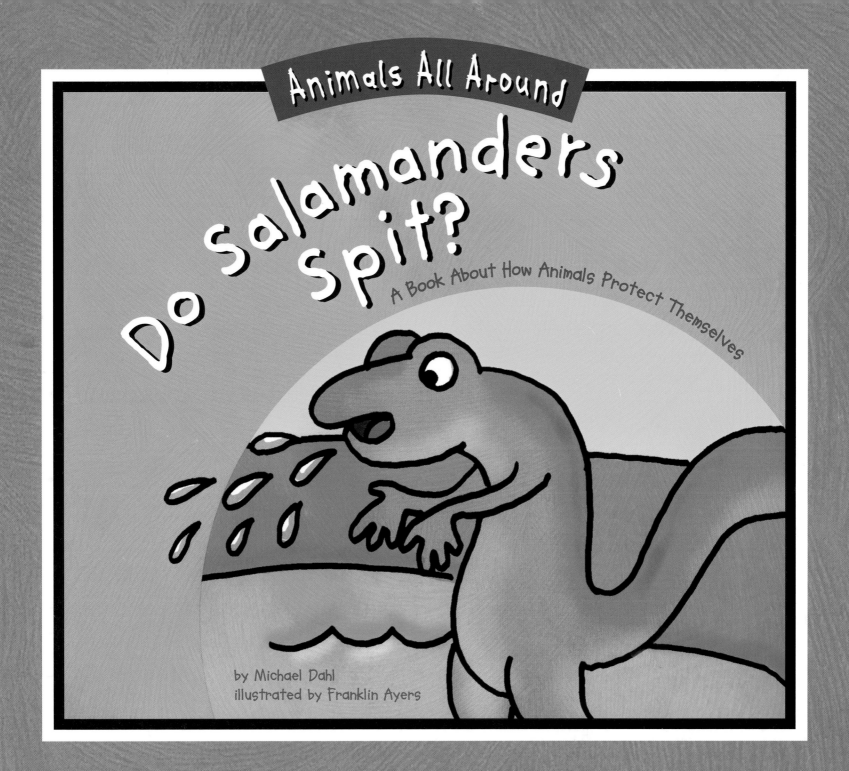

Animals All Around

Do Salamanders Spit?

A Book About How Animals Protect Themselves

by Michael Dahl

illustrated by Franklin Ayers

Special thanks to our advisers for their expertise:

Kathleen E. Hunt, Ph.D.
Research Scientist & Lecturer, Zoology Department
University of Washington, Seattle, Washington

Susan Kesselring, M.A., Literacy Educator
Rosemount-Apple Valley-Eagan (Minnesota) School District

PICTURE WINDOW BOOKS
MINNEAPOLIS, MINNESOTA

Managing Editor: Bob Temple

Creative Director: Terri Foley

Editor: Peggy Henrikson

Editorial Adviser: Andrea Cascardi

Copy Editor: Laurie Kahn

Designer: Todd Ouren

Page production: BANTA Digital Group

The illustrations in this book were rendered digitally.

Picture Window Books

5115 Excelsior Boulevard

Suite 232

Minneapolis, MN 55416

1-877-845-8392

www.picturewindowbooks.com

Library of Congress Cataloging-in-Publication Data

Dahl, Michael.

Do salamanders spit? : a book about how animals protect themselves / by Michael Dahl ;

illustrated by Franklin Ayers.

p. cm. — (Animals all around)

Includes bibliographical references and index.

ISBN 1-4048-0291-6 (lib. bdg.)

1. Animal defenses—Juvenile literature. [1. Animal defenses.]

I. Ayers, Franklin, 1962- ill. II. Title.

QL759 .D33 2004

591.47—dc22

'15

Do salamanders spit?

No! Black cobras spit.

A frightened black spitting cobra raises its body and flares its hood.
Then the cobra spits deadly poison called venom at its enemy's eyes.
The venom can blind the cobra's enemy and save the snake.

Do salamanders use claws?

No! Jaguars use claws.

A jaguar has sharp claws to slash at dangerous enemies. When the cat is frightened, its claws slide smoothly and quickly out of its paws. Its claws also help the jaguar quickly climb trees to escape.

Do salamanders curl into balls?

7

No! Three-banded armadillos curl into balls.

The three-banded armadillo has a thick, bony covering. To protect itself from enemies, the armadillo rolls up into a tight ball. Its tough outer plates of armor fit together like a puzzle. They completely cover the curled-up creature.

Do salamanders squirt ink?

No! Squid squirt ink.

Squid can swim swiftly in the sea. But faster, larger creatures like to eat squid. When a squid is threatened, it squirts ink into the water. The dark, inky cloud confuses the enemy. The hidden squid can slip safely away.

Do salamanders outrun enemies?

No! Jackrabbits outrun enemies.

A lean, long-legged jackrabbit can outrun humans and hunting dogs. It is faster than foxes and coyotes. With its powerful legs, the jackrabbit can escape a hungry mountain lion by leaping over the cat in a single bound.

Do salamanders puff up like spiky balloons?

No! Porcupine fish puff up like spiky balloons.

The porcupine fish has loose, stretchy skin. When surprised or attacked, the fish gulps in water and blows up like a balloon. Sharp spines pop out on its skin. This spiky ball scares away the fish's enemies.

Do salamanders shock?

No! Electric eels shock.

Slippery eels slide through the dark waters of South American rivers. If these snakelike fish are frightened, they will defend themselves with powerful electric shocks. Zap! Enemies are stunned and fall away.

Do salamanders disguise themselves as leaves?

No! Javanese leaf insects disguise themselves as leaves.

Green leaf insects live in the hot, wet jungles of Java. Like many other animals, leaf insects protect themselves with camouflage. Their flat green legs and bodies look like leaves, so they can hide from hungry birds.

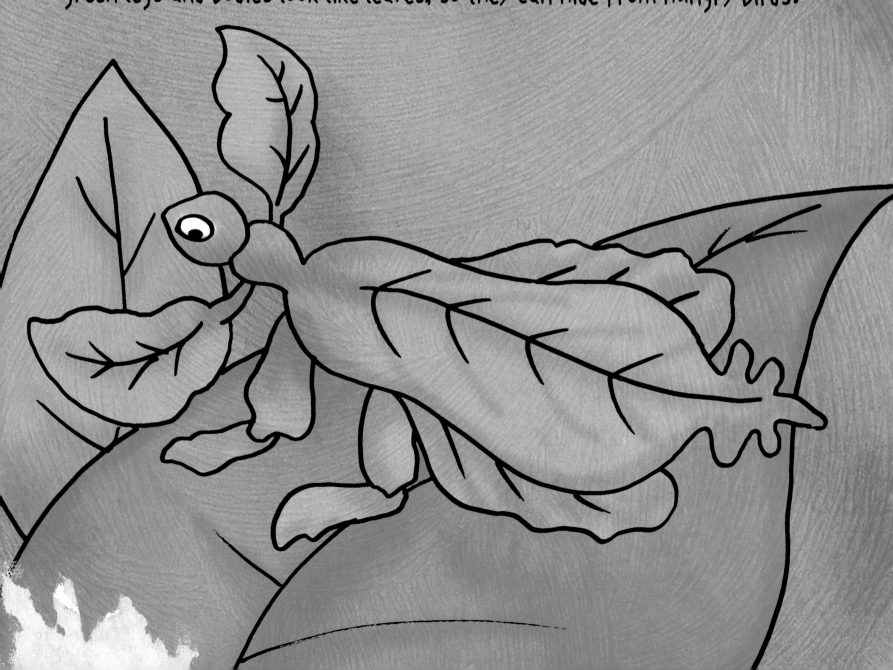

Do salamanders hide in other creatures?

No! Clown fish hide in other creatures.

Clown fish hide in the waving tentacles of creatures called sea anemones. The anemone's stinging tentacles are poisonous to other animals. But the clown fish has special, slimy skin that protects it from the sting.

Do salamanders drop their tails?

Yes! Salamanders drop their tails.

Some salamanders have a sneaky way of escaping enemies.
If a hungry raccoon tries to snatch the salamander—snap!
The salamander's tail breaks off! The raccoon is left with the wiggling
tail, and the salamander scoots to safety. Then it can grow a new tail.

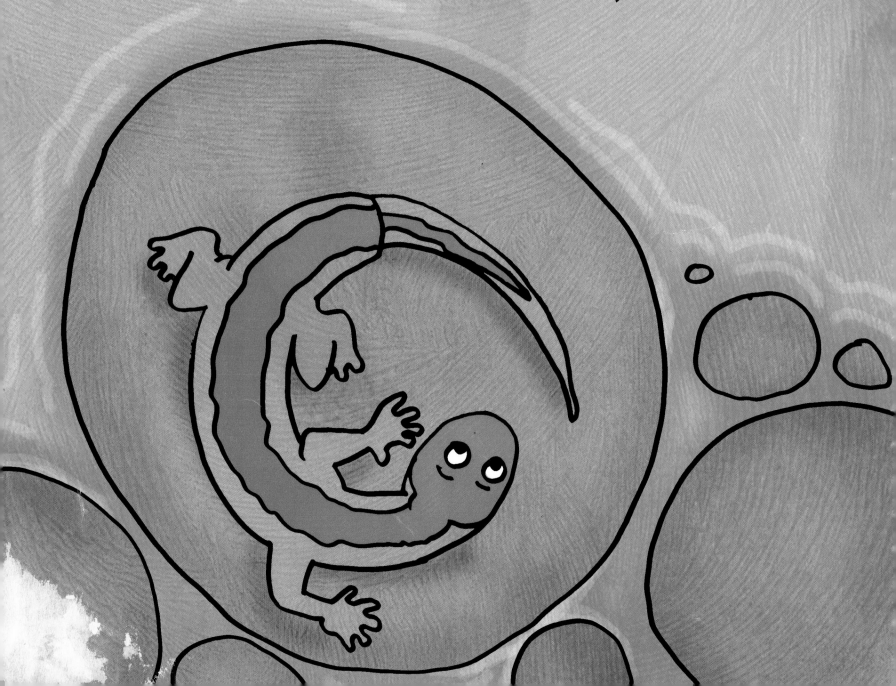

How Animals Protect Themselves

Some animals flee and escape.

jackrabbits	outrun their enemies
salamanders	drop their tails and flee

Some animals change their bodies.

three-banded armadillos	curl into balls
porcupine fish	puff up like spiky balloons

Some animals have weapons.

black spitting cobras	spit venom
jaguars	use sharp claws

Some animals disguise themselves.

Javanese leaf insects	look like leaves

Some animals use special tricks.

squid	squirt ink
electric eels	shock
clown fish	hide in other creatures

Glossary

armor—a hard covering that protects the animal or person underneath

camouflage—special covering that helps animals, people, or objects blend in with their surroundings. A leaf insect uses both its green color and its leaf shape as camouflage.

disguise—to hide by looking like something else. The leaf insect disguises itself as a leaf with its color and shape.

electric shock—a jolt of electric energy. An electric shock can hurt or even kill an animal or a person.

hood—the wide, curving sides of a cobra's head that appear when the snake is frightened. The hood makes the cobra look bigger to scare its enemies.

sea anemone (uh-NEM-uh-nee)—a sea creature that looks something like a flower called an anemone

spine—a sharp, pointed growth

tentacle—a long, narrow body part. The sea anemone has many tentacles that wave in the currents of the ocean.

venom—poison

Index

To Learn More

At the Library

Ganeri, Anita. *Extraordinary Dangerous Animals*. New York: Scholastic, 2001.

Jenkins, Steve. *What Do You Do When Something Wants to Eat You?* Boston: Houghton Mifflin, 1997.

Martin, James. *The Spitting Cobras of Africa*. Mankato, Minn.: Capstone Press, 1995.

Stone, Lynne M. *Sharp and Sticky Stuff*. Vero Beach, Fla.: Rourke Press, 1996.

Taylor, Barbara. *Scary and Sneaky*. Chicago: Peter Bedrick Books, 2001.

On the Web

Fact Hound offers a safe, fun way to find Web sites related to this book. All of the sites on Fact Hound have been researched by our staff.
http://www.facthound.com

1. Visit the Fact Hound home page.
2. Enter a search word related to this book, or type in this special code: 1404802916.
3. Click on the FETCH IT button.

Your trusty Fact Hound will fetch the best sites for you!